T0011431

Helping with Animals

by Trudy Becker

FOCUS READERS
PIONEER

www.focusreaders.com

Focus Readers is distributed by North Star Editions:
sales@northstareditions.com | 888-417-0195

Produced for Focus Readers by Red Line Editorial.

Photographs ©: Shutterstock Images, cover, 1, 4, 7, 12, 15, 21; iStockphoto, 8, 11, 16, 19

Library of Congress Cataloging-in-Publication Data
Names: Becker, Trudy, author.
Title: Helping with animals / by Trudy Becker.
Description: Mendota Heights : Focus Readers, 2024. | Series: Community
   helpers | Includes index. | Audience: Grades 2-3
Identifiers: LCCN 2023029434 (print) | LCCN 2023029435 (ebook) | ISBN
   9798889980209 (hardcover) | ISBN 9798889980636 (paperback) | ISBN
   9798889981473 (pdf) | ISBN 9798889981060 (ebook)
Subjects: LCSH: Animal welfare--Juvenile literature.
Classification: LCC HV4708 .B42 2024 (print) | LCC HV4708 (ebook) | DDC
   179/.3--dc23/eng/20230801
LC record available at https://lccn.loc.gov/2023029434
LC ebook record available at https://lccn.loc.gov/2023029435

Printed in the United States of America
Mankato, MN
012024

About the Author

Trudy Becker lives in Minneapolis, Minnesota. She likes exploring new places and loves anything involving books.

Table of Contents

Chapter 1

Walking a Dog

A boy and a dog are on a walk. They go down the street. Then, they wander through a park. The dog sniffs at plants. The boy enjoys the fresh air.

When they are done, they don't go home. The dog does not belong to the boy. The boy is a **volunteer**. He helps take care of animals. That is one way he helps his **community**.

Did You Know? Dogs have lots of energy. They need exercise every day.

Chapter 2

Animal Shelters

Many people help animals at **shelters**. Shelters are places that care for animals. Animals without homes stay there. People can visit shelters. Then, they can **adopt** animals.

Volunteers do many tasks at shelters. They play with the animals. They take the animals on walks. They feed or wash the animals. Helpers might clean up, too.

Did You Know? More than three million animals are adopted from US shelters each year.

Chapter 3

Fostering

Fostering animals is another way to help. That is when people take an animal home. They take care of it for a short period of time.

Some animals have been hurt. Foster families can give those animals extra care. Other times, shelters have no more room. They need foster families to take some of the animals.

Did You Know? Sometimes people adopt animals that they fostered.

Chapter 4

Helping Wild Animals

Wild animals need help, too. So, some people plant trees. They also let grass grow long. Those actions give birds and bugs more places to live. And they help animals find food.

Keeping nature clean also helps animals. Some places have nature cleanups. Volunteers pick trash off the ground. They clean streams. That way, wild animals can stay healthy.

Did You Know? Planting **native** plants can help animals that live nearby.

Helping Butterflies

Monarch butterflies need plants called milkweed. Monarchs drink the plant's **nectar**. They lay eggs on milkweed, too. People can plant milkweed. That way, monarchs have more places to feed. They also have a better chance of **surviving**.

FOCUS ON
Helping with Animals

Write your answers on a separate piece of paper.

1. Write a few sentences explaining why people might foster animals.

2. Which way to help animals sounds the most fun? Why?

3. What is a place that takes care of many animals that don't have homes?
   - A. a foster family
   - B. a cleanup
   - C. a shelter

4. How could keeping nature clean help animals?
   - A. They would have fewer places to hide.
   - B. They wouldn't get sick from trash.
   - C. They wouldn't come into cities anymore.

Answer key on page 24.

Glossary

adopt
To make an animal part of your family.

community
A group of people and the places where they spend time.

fostering
Taking care of an animal for a short period of time.

native
Originally from a certain place.

nectar
A sweet liquid made by plants.

shelters
Places that care for animals without homes.

surviving
Staying alive.

volunteer
A person who helps without being paid.

To Learn More

BOOKS

Hansen, Grace. *Help the Green Turtles*. Minneapolis: Abdo Publishing, 2019.

Murray, Julie. *Therapy Animals*. Minneapolis: Abdo Publishing, 2020.

NOTE TO EDUCATORS

Visit **www.focusreaders.com** to find lesson plans, activities, links, and other resources related to this title.

Index

Answer Key: 1. Answers will vary; **2.** Answers will vary; **3.** C; **4.** B